YELLOW ARROW

Vol. IX, No. 2
Fall 2024
kitalo

Yellow Arrow Journal

Creative nonfiction, poetry, and cover art by writers and artists identifying as women

Vol. IX, No. 2
Fall 2024
kitalo

Editor-in-Chief
Kapua Iao

Guest Editor
Tramaine Suubi

Editorial Associates
Meg Gamble, Alexa Lesniak, Siobhan McKenna, Elizabeth Ottenritter, Kait Quinn, and Beck Snyder

Contributors
Shawn Aveningo-Sanders, Caroline Bock, Lish Ciambrone, Maureen Clark, Daun Daemon, Kat Flores, Milan Harris, Joy Kabang, Belinda J. Kein, Ashley C. Lanuza, Lace Lawrence, ashley leshawn, Zoe Mahony, Shannon McNicholas, Jill Michelle, Luna Moore Latorre, Giselle Palacios Lopera, Ana Reisens, Sara Streeter, Iris Tang, Sarena Tien, Anuradha Vijayakrishnan, Cecilia Villarruel, Kathleen Weed, Alyson Gold Weinberg, and Cherrie Woods (aka Cherrie Amour)

Cover Artist
Liz Jakimow

YELLOW ARROW

PUBLISHING

PO Box 65185, Baltimore, MD 21209
info@yellowarrowpublishing.com

Yellow Arrow Journal - kitalo
Copyright © 2024 by Yellow Arrow Publishing
All rights reserved.

ISBN (paperback): 979-8-9883176-5-4
ISSN (print): 2688-3015
ISSN (online): 2688-3023

Cover art by Liz Jakimow (lizjakimowphotography.com). Cover and interior design by Yellow Arrow Publishing. For more information, see yellowarrowpublishing.com.

Temporary Homes
Kat Flores

How weary you must be   trekking on this journey with no end in sight
Without having a place to call home   grief
How brave you are   over and over again
Confronting things you cannot control   just stay the night

Let me take care of you now
It's dark and raining outside
Stay for the night
Stay here as long as you want
I won't ask questions
There's fresh food here and a warm place to sleep and clean blankets for you
You can continue tomorrow

I have prepared a home for you   there is a place at this table for you
A respite for your soul   a sanctuary
Still a long way to go   carry this warmth with you when you leave

Table of Contents

Dear Readers,

Thank you for spending time with this issue of *Yellow Arrow Journal* on the theme **kitalo**. As I move through the darker days, this issue feels especially resonant. In one of her essays, Audre Lorde illustrates the beauty of the dark. She believes that "These places of possibility within ourselves are dark because they are ancient and hidden; they have survived and grown strong through darkness." In my present season of life, I am reclaiming darkness and blackness as spaces of goodness—as spaces of rest, reflection, and rebuilding. The writing in these pages reflects this reclamation.

The words in **kitalo** explore familial, platonic, and romantic loss. They also explore physical, mental, and spiritual loss. Inventive metaphors abound and guide us through a world of feelings. The words within the pages of this issue shuttle us across time and space, transporting us through the Americas, Eurasia, Africa, and Oceania. They occasionally venture beyond the realism and physics of our blue planet. The words also navigate our constructed dualities of birth and death, planting and uprooting, tears and laughter, keeping and throwing, breaking and mending, silence and noise. I am heartened by the abundance of food in these pages. I believe our most universal language as a species is food; how poignant it is that we often process griefulness through our meals.

I acknowledge that the spectrums of grief and gratitude cannot be fully represented in our art, and yet, our cover artist and literary artists pushed the boundaries of this finitude. I am moved by the women, femmes, and nonbinary writers who invite us into their experiences in **kitalo**. Being the guest editor is a privilege, but the greatest gift I received in this role is true vulnerability. I grieve and give thanks alongside each of our artists here. I hope their words are lifegiving for you, just as they are for me.

Grace upon grace,

Tramaine Suubi, **guest editor**

KITALO

~kitalo~

an empathetic Luganda term
of solidarity offered
when someone experiences
a spectrum of loss that
directly translates to "this/
that is tragic" but is far
richer than that as you'll
see on the pages that follow

Yellow is Disappearing
Caroline Bock

You are going to Barcelona, giving up on this America and leaving for Spain, and *do you care about the crisis of cadmium yellow in the art world*? I ask because yellow is disappearing, and it's easier to ask about art than when you are leaving. In *Le bonheur de vivre* by Matisse, the cadmium yellow nudes are fading to ivory and will eventually be lost, a dispossessed xanthic revelry. Scientists are testing paint chips from this masterwork and others by Picasso, Van Gogh, and Miró because cadmium yellow is unstable and decomposing. Degrading. You and I know how skin chafes, pales, dies slowly, and then all at once. I don't have to tell you, Brother, I'm a reluctant traveler. We come and go, and we find that no one knows us. One time in the Bronx, I lifted you up to the open window and said *we'll see the world together*, and our mother, in one of my earliest memories, smacked my head and said *put your brother down now*. The street swayed five stories below with yellow school buses and dots of bright yellow raincoats. You were three and I was a year older, and it was all a big top of school kids and bus horns stomping between the lemon-smelling raindrops splattering our overheated apartment. We broke from the window, and I curled into you like a cat, silent, waiting; all around us, the yellows, syncopated, pulsed, alive.

You are going to Barcelona. Together, we have survived windows without guardrails and parents who needed care more than we did. After the Bronx—one day we were there with our mother, and the next gone—we had a tiny house in New Rochelle with a big garden because Pop believed in gardens more than rooms or roofs or mothers. He believed in sunflowers, though his blooms always toppled over. Their seeds scavenged by birds, his cherries by birds, his blueberries by birds. We didn't have the heart for netting or chemicals. We would have rather it all been devoured by birds. You are going to Barcelona *to discover love,* you confess, bitterly. *To make art.* You have had enough of this America. We have buried those who gave birth to us. We want to say *I love you* to one another but we've never, not once. We argue about art, sometimes politics, some days about gardens we should have tended with more care, or our parents, or some nights, lovers. *I should have slept with them all. / You should have stayed with me, at the window. / Anyways, we're off to Barcelona now, me first.* Of course, we're not. We are devoured by birds. They smell the fruit and sunflowers of forefathers and mothers on us. We are brushed with cadmium yellow, and we are temporal, fading as we are pecked at, stripped bare. *Barcelona,* we whisper to one another.

~

He's gone. For a hard split second, I don't think I am ever going to see him again. He's left me two- and three-foot high and wide pallets wrapped in a duct-taped tarp to ship to him. I tell him that *I don't know how to ship pallets to Barcelona,* and he says *we'll work it out.* And I'm sure I will. *When?* I press. *When should I ship them?* He shrugs. I have spent a lifetime figuring it out with him. In the pallets: his Christmas ornament collection, good pots and pans, Pop's portrait painted by his friend who ran the adults-only campground in the Georgia foothills—was he the friend who died of AIDS or the one of a heart attack or the one who had a seizure, tumbling into a flooded creek and drowning? Brother has a life of dead boyfriends, too. How will I live with what he has left me forever—the painting from his former assistant. When she was 19, she was in love with him, and all he could do was give her money for school in Los Angeles. He didn't know what to do with her love. She gifted him this single sad golden flower painted on a sheet of copper. He's also given me his hand-carved whale over a starry world. At night the stars on the globe, hand cut from aluminum, glint in the moonlight; the whale, a four-foot weather vane, spins, and the world's largest mammal dips, and the single sad golden flower sighs, and I think *when.*

The Five Stages of Knitting
Daun Daemon

cast on a body's worth of stitches
as if nothing has happened, perhaps
nothing has happened, perhaps
making a slip knot and working
the dangling end of yarn to make a loop,
then using the needle to pull the strand
from the ball through the loop
and then onto the needle (over and over)
means that nothing has happened
because you are starting something new,
a thing you can touch, a thing you can hold,
a thing that will take time—
don't think about time

join to work in the round,
be careful not to twist the stitches,
which could only make matters worse—
you would not be able to continue
in a fit of self-loathing,
you would have to tear it all out,
make a tangled nest of yarn, rage at the wool
defeated by fiber, you would have to start over
you. would. have. to. start. over.
you don't want to start over

after joining, work in the round,
go around and around and around
at first knitting, then purling, then knitting,
then purling, then knitting and knitting
and knitting and knitting and knitting
will it ever end? will it ever be otherwise?
will it ever only be the endless insertion
of the needle into the front loop, throwing
the yarn, pulling it through and sliding
it off the needle, automatic and numb?
you ask these questions, wanting, wanting
something different from this same—
then you get what you ask for . . .
the pattern becomes complicated

too much to handle now—
slip slip knits and yarn overs,
purling two through the back loop,
and center double decreases—
finicky maneuvers to execute smoothly,
but you must, so that you can keep going,
keep knitting, focus on the big picture,
the finished product, all the necessary clichés
you need a reason to breathe

you follow the pattern until
it is done, until it is time to let it go—
here is how to bind off, to stop
the going in circles, to close
the open loops that endlessly slide
one to the next to the next;
first you must knit two stitches,
lift the first stitch over the second one,
knit one more stitch and repeat until
you have nothing left, which is wrong
because you have made something new,
you have made something whole

I've Buried a Bouquet of Fathers
Alyson Gold Weinberg

I was only ever your daughter.

(This is the end of many things.)
You get older and your eyes veer

down at the corners.

Even so, it's you I favor.
(In truth, I look more like my

mother. I've never cared for

truth, however.) Narrative
holds my heart together.

I am sorry, I am sorry, I am sorry

I rooted around for our story.
I didn't mean to unearth the dirt

we had been lying under—

what we knew we knew we knew.
I think I will leave jars of sand

on your grave instead of stones,
so you know it's me, that I was there.

Lessons in Grief

Maureen Clark

I.
for the first time   I wonder
who was this man   my father
he is still   everywhere

in the   honeycomb calcite
the bumblebee jasper
the inkwells   full of chips of peridot

II.
every Sunday he asked
can I come and live with you
and I said *yes*
as soon as you're ready

III.
and then   he was truly gone
the hospital bed returned
to hospice

the cat still looks for him
in the living room
but   he is not there

IV.
when I have stopped
wishing
he arrives
in a dream

in my rearview mirror
as I navigate
the LA freeway
at rush hour

the whole family
filling the car
with noise
laughter

and he says
*you've got this
you've got this
honey*

Indigo

Kathleen Weed

A villanelle for Jenica 1977–1999

I write to lay wide what I do not know,
to twirl with fate, to listen when I cry.
I dip my mind in silence. The quill bleeds indigo.

I work best when a rhythm's slow.
Can ink record the music in a sigh?
I write to lay wide what I do not know.

A quiet mind has space for words to flow.
When all is dark, I blink my middle eye.
I dip my mind in silence. The quill bleeds indigo.

Mystery strums me a tune for letting go
of glib comfort, beguiling as a lulling lie.
I write to lay wide what I do not know.

We cannot keep. At best we borrow.
Too soon, the mother-luck I counted on ran dry.
I dip my mind in silence. The quill bleeds indigo.

Fierce love for you dances with my sorrow.
Let the song play on forever. I refuse to say goodbye.
I write to hold close all I do not know.
I dip my soul in silence. The quill bleeds indigo.

Death and the Hawk
Lace Lawrence

The not-yet-spring traditions of the Valley slowed my drive home that day. The pitch-black promise of the fresh-turned soil stood stark against the hazy early morning sky. The astringent residue of smudge pots hanging heavy in the air made me smile. I could already taste the cherries saved from the frost that night. I rolled my window down to take in the sweet smell of the rotting mint sludge lining the roadside like a freshly dug grave. The empty poles of hop fields rose like skeletons out of the steaming blackness. I loved seeing the land prepare itself for the changing season.

Pulling into the Ranch after such a beautiful drive, I saw the smoke curling up out of the chimney and smiled. I could almost smell the cowboy coffee and cinnamon rolls that would be waiting for me inside. The furry, earth-tone tide of lolling tongues that was always my greeting party rolled through the front yard, parting strangely around something lying just past the apple tree. My breath caught watching the motley pack skirt the remains of a Red-Tailed Hawk with a respect and fear unusual among ranch dogs. The hawk's limp body looked like the most beautiful desert sunset. Ochers, creams, golds, and gunmetal blues lit up the willow green of the grass. His head was turned with one harvest moon eye still open to the cold, blue sky. As I stared into the emptiness of what was once a gleaming soul, the earth slipped away beneath me. I don't know how long I stood there with my duffel bag in hand, dogs vying for my attention, but at some point, my mother's voice broke through the haze. "Hey, honey, what's wrong?" I pointed to the once vibrant bird now laying lifeless in the lawn, only for my mother to shrug and walk away.

Two weeks later Papa would go from having "many years still ahead" to hospice care. This honest-to-God cowboy, who I was certain could rope the moon, was dying. His still strong arms were lassoed with tubes and IVs. The barrel of his chest was swallowed by the cold white of hospital linens. Ranching teaches you too well the balance of life, so together, four generations of family waited for death to come. A week later, Papa would excitedly wake me from my watch on the tiny hospice couch. "Kitten, open the windows and the doors. I want to feel the spring!" I was exhausted, but one look at him and I couldn't help but laugh. He could never resist the first flush of spring or the last breath of fall, and I could never resist him. We spent that morning with our faces turned to the sky, the spring breeze carrying our talk of nothing in particular out toward the foothills, not knowing this would be our last conversation. Within hours, the nurses would tell us that he had slipped into a coma that he would not come out of. His rich mind, ever fertile with stories and jokes, had finally lost the battle to his body. We all stood by his side as his chest fell still. I turned to my mother for support, but all I found was cold-shouldered rage.

Red-Tailed Hawks rarely migrate, flying at most only two square miles away from their nest. They fiercely protect their small territory, and the females are known to be the most aggressive. When Red-Tailed Hawks feel threatened, they will battle, often in midair. Their talons rip into each other, and their wings beat against the other as they whirl and dive. It can leave scars that run deep. It can even kill if the wounds fester.

My mother was born and raised on the Ranch, invested in land that was never meant to be hers. As a middle child, born second to a first-born son, she knew she didn't have much of a say. But still, she stayed. She always said she stayed for us, so that my brother and I could have time with Grandma and Papa. Deep down, though, we all knew she stayed for the Ranch. The first-born son left, as did my father, leaving my grandparents to teach my brother and I how to care for this land. We fixed the fences and repaired the house, chopped the wood, and fed the animals. I came to belong to that place in a way that I have never belonged to anything else. My mother was standing in the kitchen the day Papa offered the Ranch to me, listening as he told me that he knew I could make a go of it better than anyone. I heard the skillet slam when he said he wanted to live out his days teaching me the ways of this land while looking out at the Mountain. He didn't know she was there, but I did. I turned him down. I said it wasn't mine to take but a legacy he was meant to leave to his children. When I went into the kitchen, my mother's eyes were hard and sharp as flint.

Red-Tailed Hawks mate for life. Their courtship is a breathtaking aerial display of trust and communication. During mating season, pairs will circle and dive, breaking apart and coming back together, eventually flying in perfect parallel while calling back and forth to each other across the sky. These aerial acrobatics are a testament to their bond and their strength. After they have paired, they build their nest together, sharing the role of remodeling and repairing their home for years. Even after long stretches away from each other, they will return to the same nest and wait for their mate.

As the first true blooms of spring covered the foothills, Papa was gone. His wife, the love of his life, was left behind. After folding the hospice quilt and packing the last of Papa's things, Grandma quietly returned to the Ranch and waited for death to come. This once vibrant woman, who wore bright red lipstick and gave hugs that felt like home, began to erode away. It was hard to blame her. Their love was the kind of love we all deserve and so rarely get. They met on a blind date and were married within the year. Sixty years later, Papa was still twirling Grandma across the floor. They belonged to each other. Five months almost to the day after Papa passed, the same four generations gathered around Grandma as she found her way back to him. When we went to lay her tired body to rest, I looked for the faces of the men who should carry her home, the face of the preacher who would lead us in our goodbye. I found only rolling farmlands and the Mountain in the West.

A week earlier, the generations had gathered around the mortician's table to divvy up our last responsibilities to our matriarch. Organizing the people who would act as pallbearers and scheduling the preacher had been a responsibility my mother demanded, then didn't do. I walked quickly across the still damp cemetery grass to where my mother stood, laughing with some cousins and asked her what to do. She shrugged and turned away. I moved slowly back across the cemetery to the small group left standing with the nervous mortician. "It seems it is up to us," I sighed. My sister-in-law kicked off her heels, and I stripped out of my jacket to help bear the weight alongside our partners. There were still too few of us, and we stumbled with the weight we were never meant to carry. Sweating and ashamed, I listened to my aunt speak prayers she barely remembered as a stand-in preacher, laying her mother to rest. My eyes wandered to the freshly turned dirt alongside the grave. They had covered it with a fake grass carpet, but I could still smell it warming under the August sun. It smelled like the Ranch, like home. I drifted back to the day I found the hawk lying dead on the not-yet-spring grass.

On that day a few months before, as the sun began to droop toward the hills, the Red-Tailed Hawk was still lying in the yard. It haunted me throughout the remainder of the day, popping into my view as I brought in wood, as I unloaded the car. It had become an unmoving spot on the lawn. I had not come prepared to work; this was only supposed to be a quick visit centered around the family dinner table. I thought my mother would deal with the bird. Still, it remained. I finally pulled on a pair of Grandma's old snow boots and tossed on one of Papa's work coats and made my way into the tack shed. I found the shovel with the orange handle. I knew Papa had sharpened that one in the fall, and it could break through the still hard ground. In all my years watching hawks fly, hunt, and nest, I had never seen one dead. Looking down on his body, he seemed too small to be one of the soaring, powerful birds I loved. I lifted the still beautiful bird softly with my deerskin gloves and

carried him gently to the grave I had dug under the open sunset
sky. I turned his body to the West to face the Mountain and covered
him tenderly with the freshly turned earth. I then turned my face to
the wind and let my small prayers be carried away, hoping that they
would find those who needed them.

Small burial

Anuradha Vijayakrishnan

A coffin the span of a hand does not want
much space or time.
A soft pocket of soil lined with fallen leaves
in the shade of a tree where the afternoon sun
will be a whisper, one pair of hands to hold
steady, another to dig while humming
looking away from the weightlessness
of what waited. One pair of hands to be patient
just for that little while, till it gets done.

Perhaps one kind mouth to hum a tiny
lullaby. Maybe one more to tell a story,
call out a dear name, and laugh a little
so there is no fear. Not anymore.
Not in that deep darkness full of light.
A small burial is such a small thing,
even the careless wind
slows down, pauses till it is done.

The Cruelest Month
Jill Michelle

After T.S. Eliot

isn't April—
at least for me
the wasteland comes
in the last month
the Romans made
with its unluckily even
twenty-eight days.
No burials here
no lilacs sprung
from the dead—
their two
too tiny bodies
taken for tests
then incinerated
as I wish
this grief
could be
but instead
it seeps
like February
sometimes does
beyond its
usual borders.

I am heartbroken in a Mexican restaurant again
Luna Moore Latorre

Our waitress' name is Emily,
which my mom says is a sign from God
that you are watching over me.
In my depressive pit, my first thought
is that it's just a common name,
but I don't tell my mom this,
let her hold onto the win.
My mom tells me over chips and salsa
that she is so, so sorry you are gone,
looks like she is about to cry
but instead gently rubs my cheek.
I can tell she wants to take this ugly, red tangle of hurt from me
and destroy it as water destroys fire.
The way she looks at me
like if she could drown my grief into oblivion
with a million tears,
she would sit here all night
and cry them out for me.
But all she can do is share this space with me,
keep me company in a Mexican restaurant
the way you sat with me in so many Mexican restaurants over the years,
devouring chips and salsa,
ordering two rounds of margaritas to be able to talk about
how you would have married P if he hadn't died,
how I would have married M if she hadn't broken my heart.
Both of us terrified
we would never find another love as beautiful as they were,
both of us terrified
we would never again find happiness in another's arms.

Old-growth

Zoe Mahony

There's nothing noble about all this suffering.
Men with all their things in shining black trash bags.
The last few Mondays I've been running

through the narrow tunnel and by the tumbling
sea, fast enough to temporarily outpace the whirling
whisperer inside, insistent as a heartbeat,

telling me: "You need to change your life."
When I think of the woman I want to be, who is she?
She's bringing out a massive bowl of pasta

to a group of friends clustered around a kitchen table.
She's driving through the mountains at dusk,
feeling awed by the gradient of the sky.

She cries when she's sad. She laughs when she's happy.
She has figured out how to untie her worth from her productivity.
On the weekends, she wanders slowly through a farmer's market.

She kayaks through a marsh in the morning.
Her bookshelves are full.
At the union meeting, she designs the T-shirts.

She's growing a quietness inside her,
a sparkling spaciousness. So that even shaking in fear
or surrounded by grief, she can step into love

like a grove of redwoods,
surprisingly sturdy, steadfastly tall,
burnt around the bottom,

with needles catching sunlight.

Bitter / Sweet

Sara Streeter

It is my first time being on Korean soil since I was five months old. In 1983, I was sent on a one-way flight from Seoul to Virginia where I would meet my new, American family at Dulles International Airport. Now, 34 years later and pregnant with my first child, I am in South Korea again. The experience is surreal, but thanks to the American presence that never fully left after the war, somewhat familiar. It is on this trip that I meet my birth mother and biological sisters. Like a diorama in a shoebox, the pieces are placed: a stuffy adoption agency room with worn couches, four of my blood relatives, three tissue boxes, two translators, and my utter disbelief. As someone who has never before met a biological relation, I am bewildered to see people who look like me. My birth mother's low melodic voice and the intimate, yet foreign shape of her face are disarming. As we communicate through our translators, I stare at my mother's hand clasping mine. Our hands are the same.

In the days that follow, I am disoriented. I play tourist, all while trying to package my reunion experience into something neat and tidy. It's hard enough for me to digest, let alone share with others. I stay overnight with an exceptionally kind host family in Gangnam. I'm sitting at the kitchen table when my host mother offers a persimmon from a wooden bowl. "Koreans love 감," she says in faintly accented English with a teasing smile.

I examine it. The fruit is bright, beautiful. It's smooth and supple in my hand with a slight give. The three and a half decades I spent in the United States did not include holiday persimmons on the table at chuseok or jammy 곶감 shared with my older sisters on cold winter nights. In truth, I know the humble persimmon the same way I know the woman who gave birth to me—not at all. As I take my first bite of the fruit, it's too bland, and the all-too smooth texture is unpleasant to my Americanized tongue. I'm disappointed in myself for not liking it. Besides my face, I have little else that could be deemed authentically Korean: why can't I have this? Why couldn't I enjoy 감? Doing my best to smile, I manage a nod to my host mother and swallow the mouthful. I wrap the rest in a tidy napkin and squeeze it under the table.

I am the bitter persimmon plucked from the branch.

~

When I return to the States, back to reality, I find I am no longer the same person I was when I left for Korea. Maybe meeting real, flesh-and-blood family members was more painful than the ghosts I had conjured up. I wake up in the early mornings, watch the strip of light coming from my bedroom window, and cry. When you survive so long without roots, it's hard to know what to do when you find them.

There is a persimmon tree that serves as a bridge between my family and the elderly Asian couple next door. Bountiful and lush with fruit in the fall, its branches bend over the shared fence between our two houses and into my backyard. I imagine the tree's roots lengthening and twisting beneath our homes, connecting us in a secret, unseen way. When the fruit warms to a golden ocher color in the fall, I know to wait for our neighbor. Likely the same age as my Korean mother, she walks the short distance down the sidewalk to our house. She carries a paper sack with a dozen or so persimmons, her hands worn from years of gardening flowers and cooking Thai food. I meet her at my front door where she hands me the bag. I peer in. Smiles and thanks are exchanged, her English clipped, my gratitude only semiauthentic. We wave goodbye, and I close the door. As the ritual goes, she won't return to our house again until next year's harvest.

I place the persimmons on a white porcelain platter on the dining table, admiring their warm glow and barely clinging, deep chartreuse leaves. I sigh and try one. It's still bitter, and when I taste another the following week, it tastes overripe, tangy with fermentation. I feel guilty giving them away but end up relinquishing most to curious friends. The last pieces are dumped in the compost bin under the cover of night. There, the persimmons will break down under grass clippings, broken eggshells, and slimy banana peels, gradually finding their way back into the soil from which they came.

Weeks later, clusters of fruit still hang from the otherwise barren persimmon tree. I am dulled by the wind and the heavy sky, but the fruit transforms the tree into something bright, almost luminous. The persimmons appear unsettlingly vibrant against the gray winter sky, a stark contrast to the tree's otherwise naked branches. As the season stretches on, I notice crows gleefully tearing into the remaining orange flesh, plucking the last bits of meat off the bones. The cold hurts me, though everything hurts. I want to dig a hole and sleep, but the earth is too hard. I can't reach the roots.

As spring tiptoes forward, finally showing itself, my neighbor dies, and I find her niece at my front door. She's about my age and height, with long black hair and a sad smile. We could be mistaken for family, maybe sisters. In halting English, she invites me to her aunt's funeral, and I nod, knowing I won't go. As she turns to leave, her eyes fill with tears and though we're strangers, I wrap her in my arms.

~

Time passes. I change jobs, find a good therapist, and stop crying all the time. I watch my daughter grow. I learn to live with this new version of myself, swallowing the world, both bitter and sweet.

In 2019 my youngest Korean sister and I start messaging each other on Kakao, a Korean chat app. Because we have yet to meet in person, she's somewhat of an enigma to me. It's a spring afternoon when she sends me a photo of richly colored persimmons nestled in a plastic bowl. Since she and I are strangers, every commonality we have is another minuscule step closer to one another in a distance spanning our entire lives. I would do anything to feel close to her, to understand her love for persimmons, to copy and paste myself into her memories, but even after years of sharing photos and well wishes, we are not there and may not ever be. I can claim two families on opposite sides of the globe, but I don't truly belong to either of them.

I tap out a smiley face on my phone under my sister's persimmon picture and hit send. I never tell her I don't like persimmons. I don't tell anyone.

Every now and then
Iris Tang

I visit the lighthouse
that sits atop those dagger rocks
sharp enough to cut my heart.
Most times, I walk away,
in fear, they may cut my heart.

Every now and then,
I don't walk away,
I sit beside the light-less house
on a throne of dagger rocks.
I watch as the rageful sea tosses and turns—
like those sleepless nights:
how I'm tossed and turned by my emotions.

There I spot her,
a dot of yang in yin.
Her tail shimmers even in the gloomy sky,
her porcelain face like my mother's China vase.

I know of her,
a creature of the sea, gifted with a voice,
she sings. A melody of Death they say.
I know of her,
a creature of the sea, gifted with a voice,
she sings. A show with no audience.
I know of her,
a creature of the sea, gifted with a voice,
she sings. No more.
The creature of the sea, gifted with a voice,
the gift now a curse.

I admire her,
calm as she is swallowed in chaos.
Unlike the lighthouse,
who has become light-less
just by watching the rough sea unfold.

Every now and then,
she reminds me of my parents:
quiet
until the razor's edge
cut
my pristine porcelain skin,
a gift, cracked, seems now to be a curse.
Loud:
their harmony-less symphonies cuts,
my heart, with words sharp like the dagger rocks.

Every now and then,
I put on a dress, look in the mirror, admire my efforts,
but I see my arms,
cracked.
My body comforts me
as flesh wraps around cracks trying to conceal it,
but my pristine porcelain skin is no more:
so I bury my dresses in the corner of my closet,
and change into a sweater concealing my cracks.

One day, I hope that,
every now and then,
I will try on dresses again.
And every now and then,
she will try singing again.

my grandfather's backyard
Joy Kabang

my mother tells me there were banana trees
in my grandfather's backyard,
deeply rooted
with long, lush leaves
and the sweetest fruit on this side of the Nile,
nourished by the richness of Kajo Keji's soil,
the strength of the sun,
and the wisdom inherited
by my grandfather's gentle hands.

I do not know what came
of my grandfather's banana trees
in the war,

but I know that as a child,
I took my first steps
to fetch my grandfather water
for his new garden
in the pressing heat
of Cairo.

twenty-five years
and nine homes later,
I tend to a banana tree
held by a heavy ceramic pot
on my backyard patch of
Baltimore concrete.

with each drop of water
that darkens the soil,
I think of how my family
has learned to nourish growing things
wherever we are planted. with each

new leaf that unfurls itself
and stretches toward the sun,
I thank the heavens
for what my gentle hands
have inherited. with each passing
day, my tree grows taller,

and I dream fervently
of the sweetness
she might soon bear.

And yet—

Shawn Aveningo-Sanders

How impossible it seems, here in the autumn
of my days, this unabashed joy swells up

amid sadness, as if carried by a courier
upon a hummingbird's wing. This

spring day finds me awed by a mourning dove
strutting the truss of the trellis like a circus

tightrope walker, but with less sparkle. She
is pure love personified, as she and her mate

build a nest, tucked safe beneath the new grape
leaves. From the eaves, he brings her tiny branches,

leftovers from the storm last fall. Not all of his
offerings satisfy her fastidious eye—nothing

but the best for her nest of fuzzy squabs. How
fleeting this tender moment is. A younger me

might not have noticed, or bothered to pluck
joy's plume—too scurried in day-to-day hurries.

Now as my own plumage fades to gray, I swim
in the waters of discovery, relish in the minor

wonders of my own backyard. On those days
I'm tempted to cling to my grief, when my

muscle memory bends to the shape of you
in the dark, I will whisper the day's little delights

into the night, like a lonely prayer, and tell you
I miss you . . . and yet—there was joy.

Counting Dogwood Flowers
Lish Ciambrone

Last spring, the Dogwood on the corner and I
had an understanding: Rex would stop to sniff the fence,
and I would stop to count her flowers. Four-petaled,
delicately ridged. They start out as green as leaves.

Old dogs love to take their time. Rex sniffed, I counted
green flowers going white as ghosts by early summer.
I counted them, blushing pink, turning brown, and falling
away. I counted the tiny red fruits they left behind.
Winter came. Only bare branches remained.
I counted them, too.

Rex died before the new buds opened.
I stopped walking the neighborhood.
I counted days as they passed. His hairs on the sofa.
The toys he'd left half-chewed.

Driving past the corner last night I suddenly
realized I missed her, the Dogwood waving
in a yawn-soft breeze, arms full of white flowers.
She called out to me
like so many good friends.

What else have I missed in my despair?
One loss is many, many losses,
impossible to count.
One loss, many losses, and each a chance to realize
all the ways love is just waiting for you
to lift your eyes
to see it.

Hair Care
Cecilia Villarruel

Mweneni had lost her comb, so she parted my hair with a
pencil. I sat cross-legged in the warm sand while she knelt behind
me. She said that my scalp looked like the skin beneath her
fingernails. "The pencil feels good on your head," she said.

"How do you know?"

"Your shoulders are letting go."

It was winter in Namibia, but winter is still hot. We were
sitting under a big mongongo tree. Twigs, leaves, and old fruit
shells surrounded the thick trunk, so we settled near the edge
of the leafy crown that eased the heat. Flecks of sunrays would
shimmer through the pale green leaves. Mweneni, my 14-year-old
host sister and best friend in Oshekasheka, had been teaching me
"Ekundungu," a RuKwangali song. We practiced as she plaited my
hair. She sang the first verse, and I repeated. Then, to show her that
I remembered what she had taught me, I sang the second verse on
my own.

> Kapina kupin duka
> Hagararera simpe
> Niye si kepa tasidama
> Jesuzha tuzuvha

Mweneni cupped my shoulder firmly and gave me a celebratory
shake; she was thrilled. "You are like a Namibian now!" she
exclaimed. "Now you know English, Spanish, Oshiwambo, and
RuKwangali."

There are dozens of languages spoken in Namibia and even
more dialectic variations. Because of the language diversity, many
people can speak only a little bit of a few languages. RuKwangali
was close enough to Oshikwanyama, Oshekasheka's dialect,
that Mweneni could pick it up from hearing songs on the radio.
RuKwangali is spoken in the Kavango region. Mweneni is from

Ovamboland and speaks Oshikwanyama. These regions are close to each other in the north, near the Angola border. They are different tribes with different languages, but their languages have similarities. The radio in the north plays songs from both tribes, so it's not uncommon for people to pick up songs from the other language. We went over the chorus together and then sang the whole song before falling into a comfortable silence.

I held sections of my hair while she plaited and stared out at the thin cows in the distance, the thornbushes, the clear blue, cloudless sky. The first time I came to Oshekasheka, I was worried I wouldn't find it. I had been dropped off on a tar road by a taxi driver who told me that Oshekasheka was a 90-minute walk. His directions: walk down the gravel road, turn left at the crossroads, pass a big tree next to a footpath, and continue walking until tracks from people and cars appear. "Left, big tree, footpath, track marks," I had repeated, confident that I would miss all the markings.

Now, after living for a year in the community, I knew every tree, could avoid thornbushes with my eyes closed, and recognized the sound of my colleagues' trucks from miles away. I loved it here; I loved the desert. At first, I had struggled with my surroundings, with those thornbushes. Sometimes my pants got caught on their sharp spurs, and I would yank my leg away from the scraggly shrubs, tearing my clothes. Mweneni explained that the thornbushes were used for medicine and to protect the goats. Their spines helped them survive. I softened toward the plant because I was trying to survive, too. I had gone to Oshekasheka just to get away. I was in my early 20s, the child of immigrant parents, and living on Chicago's southside. I didn't have many options at home. It was either get a job and live with my family until I could save enough to get my own place, or travel halfway across the world to teach in a remote country. The desert sounded more peaceful than home, so I left home for post-apartheid Namibia.

In Oshekasheka, I had no television or running water. My host siblings and I would fetch water once a week. I used my water

rations for drinking, bucket bathing, and washing my four dishes.
I also used it for laundry. Laundry consisted of handwashing
my clothes in a basin and hanging them on a line outside to dry.
Rolling a dirty shirt between my soapy fists under the Namibian
sun was a kind of therapy I didn't know I needed. Seeing my clean
sheets catch the wind and billow out was beautiful. When I pulled
my laundry off the line, I would hold it against my body before I
folded it to feel both the warmth of the linen and the desert sun on
my face.

I gazed out at the lovely desert as Mweneni began to hum with
her fingers in my hair. We would switch places when she was done.
When she had just a few more braids to go, we heard the ramblings
of a man approaching. He got louder as he got closer. "Oh no," I
heard Mweneni whisper. I could feel her limp hands on my head.

"It's okay. He is just drunk. Don't let it bother you."

I had seen him before, mostly at the cuca shops and sometimes
walking around drunkenly. He seemed harmless. I'd see my
students walk by him or some of the other alcoholics; they usually
just walked farther away to avoid them. Most of these men lived in
Oshekasheka or a neighboring country and were working to send
money back to their villages or their families. Many who stayed in
the community were elderly, disabled, or addicts.

When the man was just a few feet away, we could smell the
stale alcohol wafting off him. Shoeless and unsteady, he stopped in
front of us and wobbled around. He slurred words that I couldn't
understand. Then, I heard "oshilumbu" and realized he was
badmouthing me. That was the word locals used for foreigners
like me. I figured he was angry at seeing an outsider. I was sure
he'd seen me before; Oshekasheka wasn't huge, but he'd never said
anything to me until this moment. Mweneni said something back
to him that I didn't understand. I knew some Oshikwanyama, but
they were speaking so fast. It sounded like she was defending me,
but I wasn't sure. His voice rose, and he made like he was going to
throw his nearly empty beer bottle at Mweneni. I jumped up and

threw my arms in front of her. She pushed my arms down, pointed
a finger, and yelled at the man, telling him to go away (I assumed).
Was he mad at me or her? They were both quiet for a moment.
Then she inhaled and spoke calmly. I was confused by their tones
and gestures.

"Do you know him?"

Mweneni ignored my question and pointed again, seeming
to tell him again to leave. He waved his hands at the both of us as
if to say "Forget this!" and walked off. Silently, we watched him
stagger off toward the cows. He started talking to the cows as he
stumbled between them. Mweneni shook her head.

"Do you know that man?" I asked her again.

"Come, let us keep plaiting."

I sank back into the sand, and Mweneni finished braiding the
last couple of sections. We were silent. No talking, no singing,
no humming, no laughing. When we switched places, I asked if
she was OK. She nodded and sat down. Her brow was furrowed,
and her eyes seemed to search intensely for something. She was
clearly upset, but I didn't want to push her, so I just got to work. I
started undoing her loose braids, hoping she'd explain what had
just happened. But even after unwinding them all, she still hadn't
said a word. I asked for her pencil so that I could start parting and
plaiting. As I dragged the tip across her scalp, I could hear her
breathing deeply, almost like she was meditating. I wanted to ask
again, but I let it be. It wasn't until I was more than halfway done
with her hair that she finally said something.

"That man, he is my father."

My hands froze. Why had she never told me? We spoke every
day. I had asked her about her parents way back when I first learned
that she wasn't related to anyone on the homestead. She only told
me they were "away." I just assumed that they worked in a town or
neighboring country, like the parents of so many kids here. I would
have never guessed her dad was in plain sight this whole time.

"How come you never told me before?"

"It is more easy to be free with your secrets when a person is touching you but not looking at you."

"Yeah." *Like driving in a car*, I thought. I wasn't sure what to say. We were both quiet for a beat. I started on her hair again. "What were you saying to each other?"

"Nonsense. I hide from him. If I see him, I turn and go another way. Today I could not hide. Sometimes he sees me and is so very nice. Sometimes he is mean. Sometimes he says he does not know who I am. Sometimes he is loving me. Sometimes he is hating me. Today he is saying I am stealing his goats. I tell him I am not stealing his goats. He does not know who I am today. He is sick," she said, pointing to her head.

She didn't sound angry or frustrated, she didn't even sound all that sad. If anything, she sounded tired, like she had long ago understood that she would be a person who does not get to have a father.

"I'm sorry, Mweneni."

There were differences, but her father sounded a lot like my brother. He was always drinking or getting high. One minute I was his best friend, the next I was the worst person in the world and the reason for any pain in his life. Back home, there were patched-up holes in the walls from where he'd punched them. From early on in my childhood, I'd learned to read subtle clues: the sound of his voice, a gesture, a phrase. I tried to read him all the time so I could avoid a fight, so I could stay on his good side, so I wouldn't get yelled at. It was exhausting. So many times, I just wanted to disappear. I more or less did by moving to Oshekasheka.

Only for a split second did I wonder why Mweneni had never told me about her father, but then I realized I'd never told her about my brother. "I have a brother like that. He is nice and funny and makes you feel loved. Then, for no reason, he turns mean and angry and says awful things."

"He is like my father. It is confusing."

"Very confusing."

I was eight years older than Mweneni, but suddenly, I felt like a little girl again. As a child, I tried to read my brother to protect myself from him. Decades later, I would have to get a restraining order against him. I thought of my city life and Mweneni's village life. My parents did as much as they could for my brother: doctors, therapy, pills, different styles of parenting. Nothing worked. With so many resources, I had to walk on eggshells and then escape. With no resources at all, Mweneni hid. It was the best we could do. Mweneni pointed to her head again, "They are not okay."

The sun would be setting soon. I pulled a section of her hair and smoothed it with my palm. Mweneni started to hum softly. I divided the section into three thinner pieces and slid them between my fingers. I tightly threaded one through the other through the other, strengthening the bond with each intertwining strand.

Aglow in West Virginia
Shannon McNicholas

For Hannah Elliott

You've joined my memories on that hill in Wheeling
where I picked slightly soft yellow tomatoes off vines
that towered over me into the rafters of the greenhouse,

where I lay on top of the splintered picnic table,
feet hanging off the side, weighed down by steel-toed boots,
to watch lights explode into the sky, signifying independence,

where I was soaked so deep with tears from the heavens
that I swear they grabbed my heart.

This time you were there, spinning circles over the hill with me,
almost rolling down into a city blanketed by a damp, pleasant drizzle,
covered by a quilt next to blue-orange flames.

This time it was your leather soles pressed firmly to the ground,
your knees resting softly against the grass,
our sapphic glow brighter than the flames in front of us.

This is how I will always remember our time together. In Wheeling.

Everything has changed since that day.
We've grown in different directions,
I've become sober, you've changed careers.

Still, that day proves to me that love can exist in moments.

A Doctoral Education

Sarena Tien

I told my mother I'd never be a doctor
and yet here I am, performing surgery
with a stainless-steel butter knife
removing the mistakes of her new recipe
by amputating all the burnt bits

this –(ec)tomy of a cōngyóubǐng
or a green onion pancake
wasn't supposed to be part of the curriculum
for a PhD in French literature, but it's shaped me in ways
prose and language and theory have not

I needed to scrape the scabs off my identity
to find my way back to my heritage
the push and pull of belonging and exclusion
that comes with being a Chinese American daughter
who became a doctor anyways.

La abuela de mi abuela

Giselle Palacios Lopera

Quiero vivir como vivía la abuela
  de mi abuela
Con leña y café cultivado
Quiero saber como fue en ese
  entonces
Cómo fue que llegué hasta aquí

I want to live the way my
  grandmother's grandmother did
With firewood and coffee for harvest
I want to know what those times
  were like
How it was that I got to this place

I like to picture what their little
  farmhouse could have been
Made of red bricks,
  each laid by hand
I like to think of what their village
  could have been
Warm neighbors tucked away
  in the comfort of the mountains

I like to think it would get cold
  at night
They'd make their fires from
  the wood they carried home on
  their backs
I like to think about their hens
  roaming in the fields

Leche fresca pal chocolate caliente
  en la mañana
Y huevos de gallina pal desayuno

Warm milk for the hot morning
  chocolate
And fresh chicken eggs to pair

How it must have been
When being poor made you
  sustainable

They left that life to go to the city
To work in the factories
To live in the apartment boxes

My mother left that life to go
  to the States
Where every sweat and dollar was
  sent back to the motherland

When I think I'm the one my
  ancestors had been praying for
In all my riches and my power

I pray back to them
Hoping they'll walk me home
To the smells of the rivers
And the coffee beans

Whippoorwill
Ana Reisens

I've grown fond of this body
with its clever bends and creases.
The way my upper lip cracks
with laughter, the spots scattered
like stars across my skin.

Even these have begun to change.
Tell me, when the moccasin flower
wilts and the silver day fades,
what remains of us?

How precious the petals.
How precious the dust.

Yesterday, Evelyn gave her last reading.
Her fingers quivered with the page, breath
catching against her oxygen tank.
Her last word, a bird against the wind.

The flower blossoms.
The whippoorwill sings.

We stay, as long as we can,
to listen. To witness. To read
one last poem, breathe
one last breath.

Elegy in Silver
Belinda J. Kein

Last born and late for everything, that was my sister, with each
occasion, birthday, anniversary, or other cause for celebration, her
response as generous as it was slow in coming, the recipient left to
wait, anticipation part of the gift itself, building with each doorbell
ring, each delivery of any kind, each trip to the mailbox, each hand
sent inside to probe the depths in the hope that, this one time, she'd
managed to extricate herself from the chaos that was her life, long
enough to note the date, to mount a search for the greeting card
she'd surely bought, to unearth it from the morass on her desk, to
add the blue flourish of her name below hurried words of apology
and excuse, scrawled, misspelled, often illegible, the whole of it a
metaphor for her tumultuous life in the big city, all the rush and
clamor she claimed to love, so full of stress and demand, it rarely
allowed her precious time enough to seek that special gift, or any
gift at all, to wrap it neatly in crisp folds of pretty paper, ribbons
tied just so, topped by a bow, such perfection unlikely at best,
as hers were the packages that arrived with birthday paper on
wedding gifts, graduation paper on birthdays, the ribbon a ragtag
pile of recycled curlicues in colors that bore no resemblance to
the hues of the paper, more often than not, patched-up leftovers
from a previous gift, that spoke of a last-minute frenzy so typical
of her, but then, then, the long-awaited package would arrive and
there, amid the crumpled confusion of hand-me-down paper and
mismatched ribbon, as if by some miracle, would be the perfect
gift, the graceful, rust-veined, soapstone candlesticks that bore a
stunning likeness to the red rocks of Zion I hiked each year, the
lumbar pillow embroidered with words of love that supports me
still, the family heirloom ladle I'd long coveted, my admiration
coyly ignored, wrapped in a blanket of tissue, the silver lovingly
shined, years of tarnish giving way to a luminous gleam, the only
remaining darkness deep in the crevices that curled about the

slow turn of the handle to reveal a swirling cornucopia of rotund
fruits and trailing vines etched in sharp relief, rendered exactly
as in my memory, forever after evoking myriad family gatherings
and holiday feasts I'd shared with those still with us and those long
gone, my dear sister now among them, brought back to me in a
flash of silver, late as always, but spot-on.

eldest sister

Ashley C. Lanuza

dear Ate,   I learned about the multiverse
   the other day   somewhere out there, you read
     this letter and called me on the phone   together

we bled our blood into syrup

       licked the sea from our cheeks

              exhaled our abundant joy.

Our sororal symphony simmering, I gave you my bouquet of gratitude for

          being the eldest.

For weathering parental storms, finding paths along the midnight forest,

   holding me like

if there's a word for   second mothers.   Ate,

in another universe, you would have been honeydew

     —enough to push through her canal and into your life.

I miss you,   if I ever got to meet you.
Magkikita tayo.

Island Girl
Cherrie Woods (aka Cherrie Amour)

When the stress of being Black in America
Starts to overwhelm
I dig deep
Into the memories
Of my island childhood.

Where I played jacks in the front yard
And cricket in the streets.
Where I could scream and yell
With no repercussions.

Where my grandmother used
A cutlass
To cut off the head of a chicken
For our Sunday meal
And I would help to pluck the feathers.

Where a rain shower
Caused a celebration
And we danced in the rain
In our underwear.

Where when I craved something sweet
I would reach up to pick a ripe mango from one of the branches
In my grandparents' backyard overflowing with trees
Heavy with fruit.

Where I grabbed freshly laid eggs
Carefully and quickly when
One of our hens
Was momentarily distracted.

Where steelpan music played
From December to February
In preparation for
Carnival in March.

Where I excelled at both
World geography
And world history
At my local government school.

Where my brown skin
Was never a weapon
Used to
Measure my worth.

missives overnighted to aunty in the alternate universes where she might reside

ashley leshawn

care/of universe one:

On Sunday morning, the rice cooker sits open and almost
empty. Week old grains congealing, hardening, growing
mold. I live in my own house now, cannot carry fifty
pounds of jasmine rice alone across the linoleum into the
kitchen. The pats of butter melt into the countertop; Lawry's
Seasoning a solid, the shape of its tube. I close my mouth,
don't get fed.

I go to church and sit a seat away from the aisle, leaving
a pamphlet beside me so you aren't surprised by the
scripture, too. When I rise and pray over the communion,
I keep my eyes fixed on that aisle seat in case you want to
come and break bread. The Christ in me is the creator you
made, and I wait until you come back, too.

When I leave high school, I already feel you slipping from
my grasp. I write about you in my college essays to tighten
my grip. I get my license and your address is the first place
I go, swerving lanes to show you my photocopied grin.
Before dark, I pull up to your driveway, searching for you.
A "For Sale" sign greets me instead.

I look at my graduation photos and there you are, hand firmly in my grasp. You drag my belongings across the linoleum, into my dorm room. All one hundred and fifty pounds of me, draped around you. You tell my roommate you are Aunty Mary Magdalene, keeping watch for me.

I enter the sanctuary, and you have saved a seat for me. The scripture is for us, we give the sermon, and it is about the creator, our Mother, the mothers we make in each other. I don't need a Father if I have you. We break bread and Christ comes again and again.

On Sunday afternoon, we hoist the jasmine rice between us, our arms a cradle. The butter melts easy on the rice, and you sprinkle Lawry's on the top. I indulge, knowing you'll never leave me hungry.

we been been immortal
Milan Harris

Been making altars out of concrete.
Been speaking to angels on corners,
                  honoring the dead with balloons we know they see,
Comforting them with teddy bears placed at their tombs.

We been offering sips of sweet liquor to the ground,
Letting them know we still see their shadows in our minds
When we close our eyes.

We been candle lighting ourselves holy,
Whispering to God(s) to keep them safe.

We been speaking them into f o r e v e r,
Searing their memories into other people's brains,
Placing photos on tables,
On pages,
On T-shirts, so no one ever forgets that their names are still dancing
On our tongues.

We been living forever,
TraversingTimeAndSpaceAndUniversalConfines.

We been transcendent.

We been eternal.

We been been immortal.

On the Cover: Growing by Dark Rivers

Liz Jakimow

After someone I loved dearly passed away, I set myself the goal of taking one photograph a day. Photography had long been a passion of mine, so this seemed the ideal way of taking attention away from my grief, at least for a short period. I soon realised, however, that my grief was influencing my photography. I was drawn more to shadows and darkness, or cycles of life and death within nature. Rather than being discouraging, this helped me to process my grief.

The photographs I took in that initial three-month grieving period, along with poetry written during the same time, were collected in an exhibition and a book titled *A journey with grief: exploring loss through photography and poetry*. While this particular photograph, *Growing by Dark Rivers*, was taken after that grieving period and therefore not part of the exhibition or book, it was undoubtedly influenced by my grieving process.

I took *Growing by Dark Rivers* by Araluen Creek (in Australia), a place I frequent regularly that always provides me much solace and many photographic opportunities. The small plant growing by itself seemed so vulnerable, almost childlike and in need of protection. Yet it was also a strong reminder that, even in the midst of death and grief, there is also growth and hope. I may have passed by that small plant many times before. But to me, in that moment, it was beautiful and impossible to ignore.

In the editing process, I darkened the background and drew more attention to the plant while keeping the background very dark. There is often a lot of darkness in my photographs now. While some may find it depressing, it feels more authentic to who I am. Yet there are also often elements that draw attention to the light, symbolising hope.

The darkness, too, represents mystery. When a loved one dies, much time can be spent looking for answers. Sometimes the best thing we can do is accept that those answers won't be found. For now, some things remain hidden and secret. All we can do is search for the light that always reveals itself, even when times are dark.

Contributors

Shawn Aveningo-Sanders' poems have appeared worldwide in literary journals, including *CALYX Journal*, *ONE ART*, *Eunoia Review*, *Blue Heron Review*, *Tule Review*, *Amsterdam Quarterly*, *About Place Journal*, and *Snapdragon*, to name a few. She is the author of *What She Was Wearing*, a chapbook that reveals her #metoo secret after 40 years. She's cofounder of The Poetry Box press and managing editor of *The Poeming Pigeon*. Shawn is a proud mother of three and nana to one darling baby girl. She shares the creative life with her husband in Oregon.

Caroline Bock writes micros to novels. She is the author of the short story collection *Carry Her Home*, winner of the Fiction Award from the Washington Writers' Publishing House, and the critically acclaimed young adult novels *LIE* and *Before My Eyes* (both St. Martin's Press). Her latest novel, *The Other Beautiful People*, a workplace love story about a movie-loving marketing executive, will be published in the summer of 2026 by Regal House Publishing. She is also the copresident and prose editor at the Washington Writers' Publishing House. "Yellow Is Disappearing" is part of her work-in-progress, a hybrid collection tentatively titled *I Should Have Slept With Them All*. Find out more at Caroline's website carolinebockofficialauthorsite.wordpress.com.

Lish Ciambrone is a poet, painter, and personal trainer living in Baltimore, Maryland. Primarily concerned with the earthly world of bodies and plants, Lish loves dogs and cows, bodybuilders and bugs, Buddhists and Catholics, and the tall grass of her home state, Illinois. She is a winner of the Wormfarm Institute's 2024 PassWords Contest. Find her work online in *Rejected Lit Magazine*, *Bruiser Mag*, and *Peach Mag*, and occasionally on the grid (Instagram) @iamyourdad_now.

Maureen Clark's first book, *This Insatiable August*, was published in 2024 by Signature Books. Maureen is retired from the University of Utah where she taught writing for 20 years. She was the director of the University Writing Center from 2010–2014. She was the president of Writers @ Work from 1999–2001. Her poems have appeared in *Colorado Review*, *Alaska Quarterly Review*, *Southeast Review*, and *Gettysburg Review*, among others.

Daun Daemon's short stories and poems have appeared in numerous journals and anthologies, including *Flock*, *The Dead Mule*, *Delmarva Review*, *Salvation South*, *Third Wednesday*, *Typehouse Literary Magazine*, and *Amsterdam Quarterly*. Her memoir in poetry, *A Prayer for Forgiving My Parents* (Kelsay Books), was published in July 2023. Daun teaches scientific communication at North Carolina State University and lives in Raleigh, North Carolina, with her husband and three cats. When not grading papers or writing poems, she enjoys gardening, knitting, cooking, and cat wrangling. More can be found at daundaemon.com.

Kat Flores is a nurse practitioner student. She is passionate about research on social determinants of health and mental health services in underserved communities. Kat believes in the power of writing to foster empathy and healing spaces. When not pulling all-nighters, she's looking for bubble tea, mountain trails, and Greek food.

Milan Harris, formerly the director of an after-school program, now works as a researcher in equity-based education practices in Maryland. Born and raised in Baltimore, Maryland, she has always been a lover of literature. She's written for various online journals, but in 2020 she cofounded her own creative arts magazine, *Amani Sol*, with her best friend. They're currently working on their third issue. When not writing, she can be found gardening, cooking, or doing yoga.

Liz Jakimow is a photographer and poet who lives in the beautiful valley of Araluen in Australia, where she is inspired by the nature and mountains that surround her. After losing a loved one, poems and photos from an initial three-month grieving period were brought together in an exhibition and a book titled *A journey with grief: exploring loss through photography and poetry*. You can see more of Liz's photography at lizjakimowphotography.com.

Joy Kabang (she/they) is a scientist, musician, and writer hailing from South Sudan and currently residing in Baltimore, Maryland. Their poetry explores the emotional landscapes of their intersectional experiences using rich imagery and metaphor. Their poetry is forthcoming in *The Rising Phoenix Review*.

Belinda J. Kein is an expat New Yorker who resides in San Diego, California. Her work has appeared in *The Fourth River, Hippocampus Magazine, Vestal Review, The Razor*, Stanchion Zine's *Away From Home Anthology*, 2022 *DimeStories* anthology, *Mom Egg Review, The New York Times*, and *The Spirit of Pregnancy* anthology. Additionally, her work is scheduled to appear in *Belmont Story Review* and the *We've Got Something to Say* anthology. She holds an MA in English from San Diego State University and an MFA in fiction from Queens University of Charlotte. She is currently working on a flash collection.

Ashley C. Lanuza is a writer, editor, spoken-word poet, and lifelong learner. Her writing focuses on themes of cultural identity, family dynamics, and mental health at the intersections of being a second-generation Filipina American. Ashley values education and academia; she's a proud UCLA Bruin and is currently working on her master's in creative writing at the University of Cambridge. Her debut poetry collection, *My Heart of Rice: a Poetic Filipino American Experience*, can be found at your favorite online retailer. Ashley is based in Los Angeles, California.

Lace Lawrence was raised on the Yakama Indian Reservation and is deeply influenced by her family's tradition of oral history. She uses her storytelling skills to craft compelling narratives for nonprofits, memoirs, and nature-based writing. Her work has been published in *Sisu Magazine*, *Mountainflyer*, and Mountaineers Books, and she was a finalist in the 2023 Barry Lopez Nonfiction Contest. Notably, Lace is the first known person to stand-up paddle board the entire Willamette River Trail. When not working, Lace can be found out in nature with her two dogs, Trooper and Tokul, and her lime green camper van, Aurora.

ashley leshawn is a social worker and student of poetry living in Montgomery, Alabama. she has previously been published in *Simple Machines*.

Zoe Mahony (she/her) is a writer and a high school history teacher in training. She's lived her whole life in the San Francisco Bay area. When not writing poems, she can be found reading and writing queer fiction, running in the redwoods, and losing her phone at work, home, and any café she goes to.

Shannon McNicholas is a California native who somehow ended up in West Virginia and never plans to leave. She fell in love with writing poetry while attending Reed College in Portland, Oregon, but fell even more in love with the stories of people's lives. This temporarily led her out of the world of writing and into the world of social work. After traveling the country for several years working for various nonprofits, she obtained a Master of Social Work from West Virginia University. Shannon now balances her love for people and her love for poetry by writing about the stories she bears witness to.

Jill Michelle is the author of *Underwater* (Riot in Your Throat, 2025) and *Shuffle Play* (Bottlecap, 2024) and winner of the 2023 NORward Prize for poetry. Her newest work is forthcoming in *The Florida Review*, *Free State Review*, *The Indianapolis Review*, *MQR: Mixtape*, and *Pangyrus Lit Mag*. She teaches at Valencia College in Orlando, Florida. Find out more at byjillmichelle.com.

Luna Moore Latorre is a writer of fiction and poetry who lives in Southern California. Her first two books, a novel and a poetry collection, are being published and distributed in 2025 through Library Tales Publishing (Simon & Schuster) and The Poetry Box. Her short stories and poems have been published or are forthcoming in *Literally Stories*, *Eunoia Review*, *The Rising Phoenix Review*, and more. When she is not writing, Luna loves reading, dancing, hiking, swimming, and being with her cat, Da Vinci. She is 24 years old.

Giselle Palacios Lopera (she/they/ella) is a 29-year-old, second-generation Cuban and Colombian gender-creative woman from Miami, Florida. They currently reside in southern Vermont, dreaming of living off the land somewhere in the mountains. Giselle is a poet, writer, painter, advocate, educator, mental health therapist, explorer of emotions, and nervous system enthusiast. This is their first time being published.

Ana Reisens is a poet, writer, and avid enthusiast of all things winged and wild. Her poems have been nominated for a Pushcart Prize and Best of the Net, and you can find them in *The Threepenny Review*, *Crannóg*, and *The Bombay Literary Magazine*, among other places. She was born in the United States but now lives in Spain, where she enjoys long walks in the woods and is always in search of her next meal.

Sara Streeter, or 한혜숙 Hea Sook Han (she/her), is a transracially adopted Korean-American interior designer, biological mother of two, and writer. Since starting her writing journey in 2021, she has been published in *Longleaf Review*, *Hippocampus Magazine*, *Peatsmoke Journal*, and other fantastic places. Her work has been nominated for Best of the Net and Best Micro Fiction. Visit her at sarajstreeter.com.

Tramaine Suubi (she/they) is a multilingual writer who was born in Kampala, Uganda. She is a graduate of the Iowa Writers' Workshop. Her forthcoming debut is a full-length poetry collection titled *phases*, which will be published in January 2025. Her forthcoming second book is also a full-length poetry collection titled *stages*, which will be published in January 2026. Both books will be published by Amistad, an imprint of HarperCollins.

Iris Tang, or Ersi Tang, is an Asian American born in American Samoa; she is currently a senior at Pacific Horizons School, the place where she fell in love with literature. This is her second publication, the first being her poem "Smiles," published in a Pacific anthology called *Nuanua: Sharing our Stories*. Being of Chinese descent in American Samoa, her life is enriched by the different cultures. Through writing, Iris wishes to share her unique experiences growing up in American Samoa but also a slice of her life.

Sarena Tien (she/her) is a queer Chinese-American writer and doctor (the PhD kind). Once upon a time, she used to be so shy that two teachers argued whether she was a "low talker" or a "no talker," but she's since learned how to scream. Her poetry and prose have appeared in *The Rumpus*, *Snarl*, and *Sylvia*, as well as the anthologies *Decoded Pride*, *The Secrets We Keep*, and *Good for Her: An Anthology of Women's Wrongs*.

Anuradha Vijayakrishnan is a business professional living in Dubai. Her first novel, *Seeing the Girl*, was longlisted for the Man Asian Literary Prize and translated into Italian. Her first collection of poetry, *The Who-am-I-Bird*, was published in 2018 and translated into Arabic. Her work has appeared in anthologies, including the *Yearbook of Indian Poetry in English* series, and journals, including *Magma*, *Acumen*, *Stand*, *Anthropocene*, *The Lake*, and *Madras Courier*. Her poetry was shortlisted for the Erbacce International Poetry Prize in 2023. She has recently published a novella, *One Day, One Morning* (Red River).

Cecilia Villarruel is a first-generation American from Chicago's southside. She misses the widespread availability of banana seat bikes and old-timey everyday ASMR, like dialing on rotary phones. She never tires of the beauty of bedsheets drying on the line, billowing brightly in the sunbeams. She is lucky and proud to be an assistant professor in the English Department at Indiana University Northwest in Gary.

Kathleen Weed is a licensed marriage and family therapist with advanced training in loss, grief, and meaning reconstruction. She lives in the San Francisco Bay area. Kathleen's work has been published in *The Grieving Garden: Living with the Death of a Child*, *The Dead Pets Poetry Anthology*, and *All Poems are Ghosts* poetry anthology and is forthcoming in *Bellevue Literary Review*. Astonishment is the strongest emotion she experiences after having written a poem. She writes for the joy of putting the right word next to another right word and from a desire to shape what is fleeting into art.

Alyson Gold Weinberg, the author of *Bellow & Hiss*, a New Women's Voices Chapbook Competition finalist (Finishing Line Press, 2023), has poetry that has appeared or is forthcoming in *Quarter After Eight, december, ONE ART, Halfway Down the Stairs*, and *Eunoia Review*, among others. Alyson has received a number of awards for her poetry. Her prose poem "Gwen's Luncheonette" was named as runner-up for the 2024 Robert J. DeMott Short Prose Contest. Alyson is also a speechwriter, ghostwriter, writing teacher, and playwright. In her downtime, she enjoys binge-watching *RuPaul's Drag Race* with her family.

Cherrie Woods (aka Cherrie Amour) is a Baltimore-based, award-winning poet whose candid, narrative style is shared in her book *Free to Be Me: Poems on Love, Life, and Relationships*. Her poems have been published in *Paterson Literary Review, Understorey Magazine, Poet's Ink, The Fire Inside: Collected Poems and Stories from Zora's Den*, and *Maryland in Poetry*. She is working on her second poetry manuscript called *Sit Comfortably Elsewhere*.